The Heart of Grief

Kurt Borgmann

ISBN: 1-50320-938-5
ISBN-13: 978-1-50320-938-1

DEDICATION

To my siblings, my spouse, my children, and all who have walked with me through the valley of the shadow of death. My cup overflows.

CONTENTS

KURT BORGMANN

"There is nothing so whole as a broken heart."
— *Menachem Mendel of Kotzk*

"Toward all that is unsolved in your heart
Be patient…"
— *Rainer Maria Rilke*

KURT BORGMANN

KURT BORGMANN

PREFACE

A cross 25 years of pastoral ministry, I have accompanied hundreds of people through experiences of grief and loss. Here are a few of the things I have learned: One is that the church is one of the few places where people allow for grief, or even talk about it. In most other settings in our culture, grief is something to deny, cover over, or get past.

But even in the church, it's touchy. In the throes of the intense emotion of grief, we feel weak, inadequate, out of control. And we don't like that. Not at all. And while it is true that in the church we have faith and love and people to lean on, that doesn't make it easy.

I have also learned that we are all unique. The path we take is shaped by our personalities, the intensity of the relationships involved, the magnitude of the particular loss, experiences of loss in the past, and whether or not we have had time and space to grieve well.

These are things I have come to know "professionally," but when my own parents died a little more than a year apart in 2008 and then 2009 – my mom in a car accident and my dad from a heart attack – all those earlier experiences of grief suddenly slipped into a deeper place in my heart as the loss became more intense and more personal.

I felt like I had barely caught my breath from the death of my mom, when my dad was suddenly gone as well. I was not surprised at the intensity of my feelings of loss in the immediate aftermath of those two deaths, but I imagined (or maybe I just hoped) that at some point, as the years passed, the grief would fade to nearly nothing. It hasn't. Instead, it visits again and again, touching me with its continued immediacy, repeatedly uncovering the parts of my heart that are still sorrowful, and asking me to accept its new and unexpected truths.

The story of grief, I have come to realize in these recent years, is not only the story of immediate loss, but the story of longer term discovery. Grief does not end, but it does keep teaching us important things about ourselves and our loved ones. It does not fade; it just gets refocused. Grief continues to touch our lives and shape our hearts.

REMEMBERING THAT DAY

Monday, March 3, 2008

My mom called me in the morning to help her put away the Christmas decorations. She told me that my dad, who had recently had abdominal surgery, was not up to the lifting and carrying. I knew she had a second agenda – to see her pre-school granddaughter Leyna, who spent every Monday with me on my day off.

We went over to their house. My dad played with my daughter while my mom chatted with me as I put boxes away in the attic and garage. An hour and a half later, with kisses and hugs shared between Leyna and her grandparents, we said goodbye.

By the end of that day, my mom was gone.

My wife and I were already in bed when the call came from the Sheriff's department around 11 pm to tell me there had been a serious car accident. By the way he said "serious," I was pretty sure one or both of them were dead. Eventually he confirmed that my mom had died and my dad had been taken to the hospital. He couldn't confirm my dad's condition, but offered to meet me at the emergency room.

We decided my wife would stay at home with our sleeping children, so my pastoral colleagues – my friends – drove me to the hospital. In the emergency room waiting area, the man who had called from the Sheriff's office, who now identified himself as being from the Coroner's office, handed me my mom's purse. I could still hardly believe it, but when I held the purse in my hands instead of seeing it hanging from my mom's shoulder, I knew it was true.

As I think back, part of what still troubles me is the mystery of what actually happened. I search for and hold tight to details about their movements that day, since, in grief, so much seems unfinished and unknown. We know my parents went to town in the late afternoon for a doctor's appointment for my dad. They went out to eat, shopped for groceries. By the time they headed home the light freezing rain had turned to snow, with plenty of wind.

Coming over a rise in the road, my dad inexplicably crossed the oncoming lane, went off the road, and the car rolled over before coming to rest upside down in a ditch.

There were no other cars involved, but those arriving first on the scene reported the accident was horrific. My mom was killed immediately. My dad was transported to the hospital, in serious condition. My mom's body was taken directly to the morgue.

What happened? Did the car just slide out of control? Did something surprise my dad? Distract him?

The police reported that neither of my parents was wearing a seat belt. Impossible. My dad was a fanatic about wearing seat belts.

But later on, my sister and I went to see the wrecked car. We needed details to clear up what made no sense. We discovered that the seatbelts had not been cut to free my parents' bodies from the crushed car, so either they had not been fastened or they had failed to stay secured.

What happened? I've tried a dozen scenarios, until I've settled on this: My mom is tired, so she reclines her seat. That puts the seatbelt across her neck, so she unfastens it. My dad's sore abdomen prompts him, this one time, to make an exception.

As they come over the rise, perhaps a deer crosses the road at that moment – like the three deer I encountered at the exact same spot just a week after the accident when I was coming home late after visiting my dad in the hospital.

A deer steps out, my dad tries to avoid it, the car slides off the road, and in an instant everything changes forever.

GRIEF IN ITS BEGINNINGS

Wednesday, March 5, 2008

Dear friends,

I want to share the news with you about the car accident my parents had Monday evening. They were traveling home from Fort Wayne during an ice storm and went off the road. My mom died at the scene and my dad is in critical condition. Below is an update.

Kurt

****

My dad was moved today out of ICU onto the regular neuro-surgical floor of Lutheran Hospital in Fort Wayne. He has broken bones in his back and neck, but nothing requiring surgery. He also has bruising on the brain, something to watch.

The best way I can describe him is that he is foggy and tired and he has a lot of pain all over. It may be many weeks before he comes into a more clear space mentally, but we are hopeful. He can answer some simple questions, but he is not able to have a conversation and he does not initiate questions or comments, so he still does not know anything about what has happened to my mom.

As we wait for him to recover more, we have to postpone a memorial service for my mom. She will be cremated. It may be as long as six weeks or more before we can have a service, but when we do, it will be here in North Manchester.

Your love, prayers, and concerns are so appreciated. My brother Kevin and my sister Karin are here too until Saturday, and then will come back later to offer presence and support. We are making our way through all of this the best we can. It's still a shock.

love to all,
Kurt

Sunday, March 9, 2008

Sermon: "True to Your Heart"

When Mary came where Jesus was and saw him, she knelt at his feet and said to him, "Lord, if you had been here, my brother would not have died." When Jesus saw her weeping, and the Jews who came with her also weeping, he was greatly disturbed in spirit and deeply moved. He said, "Where have you laid him?" They said to him, "Lord, come and see." Jesus began to weep. –John 11:32-35 (NRSV)

This morning, before I sermonize, I need to say a few things about the events of this week and the circumstance of my preaching this morning. Since it has been talked about in various places, and even mentioned for prayer this morning, I feel safe in assuming that all of you are aware of the horrific car accident on Monday that took my mother's life and seriously injured my father, who continues to be hospitalized. Those things you know, but there are some other things I want to tell you about this preaching moment before I begin:

First, both you and I know that I am full of emotions right now – shock, grief, and uncertainty, to name a few. Those emotions may leak out a bit this morning, and what I am really hoping is that by saying that my emotions might leak out (okay, even pour out), that I'll keep it from happening – sort of like carrying an umbrella as a hedge against the rain.

Second, I want to say that I love all of you and I am deeply grateful for your prayers and your presence in so many ways with me and my family.

Third, I want to say that I am preaching this morning not because I have to, but because I want to. I could have asked not to, and my kind and generous colleagues would have taken up the task in a minute, but thinking through this sermon and the connections between the text and the unfolding of life has been important and helpful, instructive and even healing – for me anyway, and I hope it might be so for you as well.

Now to the sermon.

The question for the first Sunday in Lent was "Why are you here?" The second Sunday, it was "Where do you come from?" Then "What holds you back?" And last Sunday, "What do you know?" I settled on this week's question more than a week ago, so it's ironic that today we have the Lazarus story coupled with my experiences this week.

The question is, "What makes you weep?"

I dreamed about my mother on Tuesday night, not much more than a day after she died. I dreamed I was talking to her – just about normal things. And then I woke up.

What makes you weep?

We kept a constant vigil for my dad for just a couple of days before they moved him out of intensive care. But during that time we learned to know the stories of others who are still waiting there outside the ICU – one woman whose son is in a medically-induced coma following a car accident; two weeks have passed and there are no signs of improvement. Another family waits on a husband, a father, who has a brain tumor, and now a life-threatening infection in his brain as well. One woman who was waiting told us she has been coming there to be with her loved one for 45 days in a row.

What makes you weep?

On Monday morning, the day of the accident, Leyna and I went over to help my mom before she and my dad went to Fort Wayne. She wanted me to put away the boxes of Christmas decorations – boxes and boxes! As I hoisted the last one up onto the high shelves in the garage she said, "When I'm gone, no one will want all this stuff." I didn't say anything.

What makes you weep?

Emails – dozens of them – from you, from other friends, even from people in the community. And calls and visits and food and cards and offers of "anything we can do." How can so many people care so much? It is overwhelming.

What makes you weep?

The unknown. Sudden death. That although I often did, I didn't kiss and hug my mom the last time I saw her. That she won't see my children grow up. The sadness and shock on my dad's face when finally we were able to tell him that she died.

What makes you weep?

Jesus comes late to the scene of Lazarus' death. Mary and Martha are deep in grief over the loss of their brother. And quite frankly, aren't they angry? At least Martha seems to be. She comes to meet Jesus before he gets to the village. We can imagine her hurried stride and then her clipped words: *Lord, if you had been here my brother would not have died.* Those words can be read, I suppose, as her simple statement of fact, but I can't help hearing the accusation in them. Jesus delayed, and now Lazarus is dead. And everyone's hearts are broken. But then her words seem to turn – toward pleading: *But even now I know that God will give you whatever you ask of him.* As in – *You can do something if you want to. Don't let this happen. Make it turn out differently.*

Just a few moments later, Jesus is headed into the village to see Mary. And Mary says the same thing her sister said moments before: *Lord if you had been here my brother would not have died.* It would seem the sisters have talked. Where is Jesus? Why hasn't he come? He could heal our brother…why hasn't he come to do what he can do? Doesn't he care?

The gospel writer, of course, frames the whole story as an opportunity for God's glory to be revealed. Jesus even says as much earlier in the chapter. But there's something else revealed, and it's right after Mary says in effect, Why didn't you come? Where have you been? and then begins to cry.

This is what the text says: *When Jesus saw her weeping, and the Jews who came with her also weeping, he was greatly disturbed in spirit, and deeply moved. He said, "Where have you laid him?" They said to him, "Lord, come and see." Jesus began to weep.* Or as it says in the more concise Revised Standard Version, *Jesus wept.*

Jesus wept. It's the shortest verse in the Bible, I've heard. Perhaps we could say that on a per-word basis, it is also the most compassionate verse in the Bible. Jesus wept.

What makes you weep?

Pain. Despair. A troubled spirit. All those things that move you deeply. Jesus wept and we do too. It is the evidence of our common humanity, our common heart; not the glory, but the grief.

And what are those things that move us to tears? They are the deep things of our lives: the relationships we hold most dear; the connections lost or regained. It is separation; it is reunion.

I suppose it could be argued that this chapter in John's gospel is really about the glory of resurrection. It's a story about life renewed and reclaimed. But for me it's as much a story about compassion and empathy and tears and heart. Jesus may be true to his mission – that is, as John describes it, his mission of revealing the glory of God – but that does not make him heartless. He sees and hears the weeping, the grief, the pain of life lost, and it not only disturbs him, it moves him to tears of his own.

What makes you weep?

It is always that which moves your most human heart: not only your own pain, but the pain of another; the loss of relationship; the loss of presence.

But in the context of the gospel story (much less the context of our own lives), does this really change anything? Is Jesus' sympathy and grief true enough to make a difference in the story or a difference for us? After all, before the end of the chapter everything is back in line again, right? Lazarus is raised from the dead; death is overcome; loss is redeemed by restoration of life. So are Jesus' tears real? And do they really matter?

I say yes. God chooses to enter our pain, and not because we have somehow forced the issue or pulled the emotional strings. And Jesus himself, in raising his friend Lazarus from the dead, not only sets in motion the events that will lead to his own death, but breaks open once more that most human and divine of qualities – the quality of heartfelt empathy. Perhaps we can't prove that this is the case, but we sense that Jesus, in his own tears, is not playing a game or manipulating an audience. Somehow we know that his weeping comes from a place where he is truly touched – "disturbed," the scripture says — by the pain and profound sense of loss that Lazarus' death has caused his dear friends. And we know that because when we are being true to our own hearts, the same is true for us.

I wrote this sermon in a hospital room this week. Mostly just in the presence of my slowly healing father and one or both of my wonderfully present siblings. But we were not alone. I am clear about that. If it is in fact even possible to feel the tangible presence of prayer, then I would say I felt it. If it is possible to be bathed in the empathetic tears of others, then I was so bathed. And I think Jesus has been present as well, weeping as I have wept and some of you have wept with me; present in us and between us in ways that we don't yet fully comprehend.

What makes you weep?

On Monday, the last day I saw my mom, she meant to send home with us the last of her Sand Tarts — our favorite family Christmas cookie. I forgot to take them along, and when I went into my parents' home the day after the accident, I saw the container of cookies there in the kitchen counter, my name on a piece of masking tape she had taped to the lid. I took them home.

Friday morning, we packed a couple of the cookies in my son's lunch for school. My daughter, sitting in the high chair for her breakfast, saw them and pushing her breakfast aside, called for a cookie. I held the container for her to choose. Carefully she examined each one, and then chose the one with red sprinkles. She ate it with a big smile on her face. After all, how often do you get cookies for breakfast?

What makes you weep?

Sometimes the very same things that make you ache with gratitude.

Lazarus is dead. Where were you?

I'm here now. It's okay. I'm here.

In every pain there is presence. In every death there is resurrection. And in all times, Jesus is with us, in his tears and in his glory. I believe it is true. I believe it in my heart.

Amen.

Tuesday, March 11, 2008

Karin and Kevin,

Details and details. I want to update you about three phone conversations I've had this afternoon.

1.) I spoke with the coroner about Mom's missing engagement ring (Grandma's ring) and asked him to check the inventory list or photos taken to determine if it was on her hand at the time of death. I also asked him if they had any of the zip bags she commonly used to keep her medications, thinking that it might be possible that she had placed her ring in one of those. He will get back to me. If it was lost from her hand during the accident, we won't find it. I just wanted to follow up.

2.) The auto insurance claim agent said he received the police report indicating neither Mom nor Dad were wearing seat belts, so they are not eligible for the $10,000 additional death benefit.

3.) The admissions person from Timbercrest (the facility where Dad might go for further care after discharge from the hospital) called me. They are trying to deal with some obstacles related to receiving Dad, specifically around caring for his dialysis. They need several (as many as six) nurses to be trained for this, and that means training in Fort Wayne. Also, it is possible, she said, that Medicare won't pay for the dialysis equipment and they (Timbercrest) will need to eat that cost. Like I said, obstacles, but they're still working on things. If and when (I hope it's "when" rather than "if") they are ready to receive him, the hospital is ready to discharge him.

Dad is still recognizing me (and Loyce today) and he is able to indicate his preferences when I ask, but he's not asking questions or initiating conversation. He doesn't remember the accident or the days before, and he also doesn't remember that the two of you were here last week.

Not much news to encourage you, but that's all for now.

love,
Kurt

Wednesday, March 12, 2008

Karin and Kevin,

Dad has had a pretty good day, I think. He's not eating a lot, but some. At lunch time, as I was feeding him, he looked up at me and said, "Is this the routine?" I told him yes and explained again to him what was going on each day, particularly with respect to his various recovery therapies.

Later, I was rubbing his head (his hair, his scalp), and he looked at me and said, "I have a feeling that this is what it means to be treated with tender care." I said, "What do you mean?" He said, "This touch is gentle and tender." I said, "Who else has given you tender care?" He said, "My mother. My father. My children. But most of all my parents."

I don't know why he didn't mention Mom. Maybe at some level he's blocking out what is too painful to consider, or it's just too hard to say her name, or something else. Anyway, today was the first time he's really initiated any conversation with me.

I'm still standing in the middle of this discharge conversation – I had a lengthy talk with the dialysis nurse today who said he will have to go to a nursing facility for the dialysis care, and gave me another suggestion if neither facility in North

Manchester can take him. No word back yet from either Timbercrest or the hospital social worker.

love to you both,

Kurt

Thursday, March 13, 2008

Dear Karin and Kevin,

What a day. When I arrived around 8:30 am, Dad was just finishing breakfast, which he promptly threw up (including the potassium he had taken orally). What a mess.

Then mid-afternoon, he had what the neurologist called a "focal muscle seizure" on his left side, starting in his leg and moving up his side into his chest. It was quite a scary couple of minutes. When I left this evening, they were rolling in equipment to do an EEG and tomorrow morning early he'll have a CT scan. I'll go in first thing to try to be there when the neurologist makes his rounds.

I should also say that Dad is making what I think is pretty good progress in his awareness and in his initiative to talk and ask questions. He makes more expression when he's in pain or unhappy about something.

When I went over to Mom and Dad's house this evening to put back tax papers and just check on things, I sat for a while in Mom's chair. It was so quiet there, and sad. It feels like she should be there, but she isn't. Just echoes of her. I think of all the times I walked in to find her sitting in her chair.

I hope you all are okay. I think I am finding this harder, not easier as the days pass.

Kurt

Saturday, March 15, 2008

Karin and Kevin,

Dad did much better with his eating today. No therapy. He was pretty quiet and subdued most of the day – didn't respond much to questions or physical stimulation.

After dinner he seemed more alert, so I showed him pictures and talked about the grandchildren. He could remember and identify Benjamin and Rainer on his own, but not the other grandchildren, although he repeated their names as if he knew them. When I came to the last picture in the book, the one of him and Mom, I asked "Who is this?" He just looked at it awhile and then said, "I don't know" and looked away. Also, I asked why he's there. He said, "I had an accident." And then asked me why. I told him he hit a patch of ice on the road and went off the road. He repeated that several times, "The road was icy and I had an accident."

love to you,
Kurt

Sunday, March 16, 2008

Karin,

In response to your email question from yesterday, no plans for his birthday. I talked with him yesterday about it. I said it was March 15. "What does that mean tomorrow will be?" He answered, "My birthday." I said, "Do you want anything for your birthday?" "No," he said. Then he thought a moment and said, "Maybe some music."

If you want to, we can do something after you get here. What is the timing of your travel plans?

Kurt

Monday, March 17, 2008

Karin and Kevin,

Dad remains in the hospital. Perhaps with coordination with Timbercrest worked out tomorrow, he will be released.

This afternoon he was pretty talkative. He kept asking "What is the benefit of this?" and then said things like, "The benefit is learning...learning from our mistakes...learning from our accidents." He also talked about the "miracle of healing" and the knowledge we gain through things like this. The words were typical for him, but the thoughts were only partially formed and not always logical. It was like he was trying out some thoughts and wanted to see if they worked.

When I left, he seemed disappointed that I was going. Most of the time he talked I had been sitting on the edge of his bed, and he either held my hand or held on to my arm. He's trying to make connections. One other thing...at one point he said, "I will make every effort to..." (long pause) I asked, "Every effort to what?" "I will make every effort to..." I was waiting for something profound, but the next thing he asked for was a bed pan. Oh well.

Kurt

KURT BORGMANN

GRIEF SETTLES IN

Monday, May 5, 2008

Karin,

Yesterday evening, I brought Dad to our house to celebrate Rainer and Konrad's birthdays. When I took him back to Timbercrest, I waited while he used the bathroom, and as I was looking at the digital pictures of Mom, I started thinking about how she should have been with us at dinner, and the tears started to come.

When he came back in the room, he asked me if it was about Mom, and I said yes, and he started to cry, too. Then it just seemed to come in waves for him. He said he thought he hasn't really been able to grieve until now. It has all seemed so unreal so long as he is at Timbercrest and not yet home.

I think it's definitely time for a memorial service.

Love,
Kurt

Tuesday, June 17, 2008

Karin and Kevin,

Friday: We went to Dad's appointment with the neuro-psychologist. The doctor did not impress me much; she just seemed like a chart and test person, without much curiosity about Dad's situation, though he seemed fine with the experience, noting that it's something he just needs to walk through in order to return to his goal of receiving the training to administer his own dialysis.

Sunday: Dad didn't come to church, but he did come to our house for Father's Day. He was pretty quiet, but appreciative. He was pleased when I invited him on Saturday, noting it would be the highlight of his week.

Monday: I took Dad to his ultrasound appointment -- nothing new, and no blood clot was detected.

Today: I brought Dad over to the church this afternoon to plan for the memorial service as well as just to talk about memories and reflections. Loyce joined us as well. Dad had made a list of things he wanted to mention about Mom, so his thoughts were well organized in advance and he was able to come along and carry his part of the conversation. I did notice he is still slow to process new information -- he needed to hear the order of things for the memorial service events a couple times to get them straight in his mind. He was grateful for the chance to talk at length, but also embarrassed at his "weakness" (his word) because he came to tears at various times. We also looked over the Memorial Garden at the church which he hadn't really looked at before.

Dad seems to understand and accept staying at Timbercrest for at least another month. I know he's watched some Euro Cup soccer this past week, and enjoyed that. This is a better "stage" than the last one, for certain. Also, Karin, he really appreciates the grief book (*On Grief and Grieving*, by Elizabeth Kübler-Ross and David Kessler). He carries it around with him when he goes any place.

love to you both,
Kurt

Sunday, June 29, 2008

Sandra Borgmann Memorial Service Reflections

For what seemed like a long time after my mother's death – although it was really only a couple of months – it felt to me like she had just vanished. I would come into my parents' house to get something for my father or to water the plants, and I'd come around the corner from the hallway into the family room, where she so often sat to do her handwork, or clip recipes, or watch sports on television, still expecting to see her sitting there. I *knew* she wouldn't be sitting there, but for weeks and weeks I couldn't shake the feeling that she *should* be sitting there. But she wasn't. It was as if she had vanished. In the days after she died, I sat a few times in her chair. For a little while there was still the lingering scent of her there. But too soon that was gone as well.

I sorted through pictures and printed some and put them into frames to sit in my office. And other pictures I put into a computer file and made that my screen saver so that if I turned away from my computer for a while, when I turned back, there would be a procession of pictures crossing my screen. And even so, even with reminders in front of me, I still felt like she vanished.

One morning she's here, and I'm helping her put away boxes of Christmas decorations on March the 3rd (and that was so typical of her – stretching out Christmas as long as possible, and then some…) and by that evening, she's gone.

A couple weeks after her death, I wanted desperately to talk to her – not about anything important, just to talk. And some well-meaning person suggested that I just do that – just talk and she would hear me. But I couldn't do it.

And then about a week or two ago I was in back of my parents' house in their garden picking some strawberries in the evening at dusk, and I crossed over to something else. Something shifted. I think it was in the picking of the berries. My mother loved strawberries. If you put everything else in the world in front of her along with a bowl of fresh strawberries, she would have chosen the berries.

So I was there picking berries and thinking about how much she loved them, and the sun was going down, and the mosquitoes were starting to get me, and I hurried along, picking as many of the small red berries as I could find in the far bed. But then something in the near bed caught my eye, a glint of red in the fading light. I lifted a leaf and there was the biggest berry, and then as I searched, another and another. Huge berries – as big as any you can find in the store, the sort that are shipped from far, far away. But there they were right in front of me. And I realized there in my mother's strawberry patch was the exact opposite of what I had been feeling. Instead of her vanishing, there was something of her appearing. It was unexpected and yet so entirely predictable. Of course there would be more strawberries, more than I expected, more than I could see at first.

And I picked until I couldn't see at all anymore and I realized as the sunlight disappeared that there were still more to be harvested. I would have to come back the next day. And it seemed to be an affirmation that my mother didn't vanish; that there are glints of her life and the plantings of her life all over the place.

Some of those things are in me; some are in you; some are in the garden behind her house; some are in the values and beliefs and expressions of her life embodied in the church; some are in the heritage of family – those who have passed before us, those who are yet to be born, and all of us who are alive today; some have been seen and heard and spoken of and will even be tasted here today. And all of those things are as red and ripe as those berries behind her house.

My perspective on life has changed significantly since the beginning of March. Some things matter more. Some things suddenly matter less. Fewer things seem in my control. There is less that is predictable. But I'm realizing finally that I am still harvesting the fruit of my mother's life. And I do it gratefully because I know that even that doesn't last. Everything has its season. But for now, the berries are accessible and they are abundant.

KURT BORGMANN

GRIEF LINGERS

Sunday, November 30, 2008, First Sunday in Advent

Sermon Excerpt: "I sure didn't see that coming"

"Be aware, keep alert; for you do not know when the time will come."
—Mark 13:33 (NRSV)

It's a strange line from a strange text to hear on a Sunday when we are kicking off what many people consider to be the most tradition-laden, event-predictable, pattern-conforming time of the year.

Be awake? Keep alert? We don't know when the time will come?

Come on. This is a season perpetually measured in terms of "shopping days remaining until Christmas." It is highly predictable. We know what's coming. We even know when and how and with what baggage it will come. Money will be spent. Gifts will be given. Food will be eaten. The only mystery is how much money, how many gifts and how much food.

So, maybe the yawn we stifle at being told to be awake and alert in this season of Advent is because we *do* expect it to be so predictable – even in terms of the Jesus story.

That is, we don't think of Jesus in this season so much *returning*, as we think of him as being *re-played*. So the warning and danger of this 13th chapter of Mark doesn't stick to us or with us. In our memories and expectations, Jesus comes wrapped in swaddling clothes, not "in the clouds, with great power and glory." Hush, little baby. There's no need to stay awake.

There are some who *do* think about Christ's coming again, instead of Christ coming once upon a time or Christ coming in our remembering. There are some who study history and the heavens to pinpoint the timing of a rapture. There are some who are watching for Jesus to come in power and glory. There are some…but not many, at least not in our circles, and certainly not in the broader, secular Christmas culture.

No. If we are at all alert, it is because we are painfully aware of our personal uncertainty, not the possibility of a darkened sun and moon, along with the stars falling from the heavens. Even at that, we dare not be fully awake, and give full expression to our suspicion that if we are *too* alert, we might invite some dreaded, dramatic explosion of our reality.

No, on this first Sunday of Advent, we aren't ready for Christ in the clouds. We aren't even awake. And truth be told, we don't like or want anything to jolt us in these weeks leading up to Christmas.

Take this morning: How many of you liked the blank page in your bulletin where the order of service is usually printed? You didn't know the scripture text or the sermon title or the hymns. How many were excited and delighted at having to pay closer attention, having to stay on your toes, not knowing what was coming next, or even when it would all be over?

Nobody likes to be awakened from a slumber, especially for what is not anticipated or predicted. No one wants to be shaken from a quiet, comfortable sleep.

At our house, I'm the only one who sets an alarm clock, and my clock is set to music – the same track from the same CD every morning. Just a few bars of one of Nora Jones's gentle and almost dreamy ballads. It's enough to stir me from sleep, but not so much to shock my system.

Others in our household require first and second notifications. Some can tolerate no more than a sliver of light, a rub on the back, but please: No words!

And staying awake? Staying up is not a foolproof strategy for warding off danger or preparing for the unexpected.

The night of my parents' car accident and my mother's death, I was asleep when the call came after 11 pm. The ringing of the phone ripped me out of my sleep, as it always does when I have settled into something deeper than just drowsiness. Until I come awake enough to process the sound of the ringing telephone, my heart races. That may have to do with taking calls in the night that don't bring good news, but it is also a physical reaction to the jolt of being wakened suddenly.

My first thought that night was that my mother was calling with some question or tidbit of information. She sometimes forgot how late it was.

Instead, it was the sun darkening and the stars falling.

After that night, for months, I found it harder to rest. Almost every night I expected the phone to wake me again. And while I was awake, I was edgy with the kind of anticipation that's tinged with uncertainty and worry.

It has made me realize, in a way I never had before, that one way of being awake, is being hyper-aware that no matter how much we try to organize, or anticipate, or predict, or control…we can't. We don't know what's coming next. We just don't know.

This first Sunday in Advent, do we know what's coming in these next four weeks? Do we know how we'll feel? What will happen? What we will lose and what we will gain? Where we will end up by Christmas Eve?

No, we can't know these things. Even being awake does not guarantee the gift of foreknowledge. But there is this question: Will we pay attention anyway? Will we stay alert? Will we take some things off autopilot and really *feel*, *watch*, and *experience* our losses and our gains, our steps and our direction? No sleepwalking. Awake. Alert.

The scripture isn't suggesting we need to be ripped from sleep, but neither can we doze this season, or any, for that matter.

This year I lost one of my illusions – the illusion that life is predictable. I thought I was paying attention, until I realized that wishing things to be a certain way and seeing them as they are, aren't the same thing. I learned I have to stand in the moment and watch it and meet it and accept it and live it. Who knows what's next?

Wednesday, December 3, 2008

Reflections for Congregational Luncheon

Thanksgiving was welcome and unwelcome in my heart this year.

I was gathered with not only my wife and my children, but with my siblings and their children; and my father too: the extended family of my adulthood. And for that, this year especially, I was truly grateful.

At the same time, the holiday was unwelcome because it provided an intensely unrelenting, unspoken, and yet completely tangible reminder of what will never be the same again since my mother's death almost nine months ago.

Even that span of time – nine months – falls onto me with symbolic irony. Nine months is the time of gestation, or pregnancy, of anticipation of a new life. My last nine months leads where? To a place that feels darker now than it did in mid-summer. The urgency of holding things together through those first months, of tending to my father and focusing on his recovery, has faded. And in its place, just the dull darkness of grief deferred and a place without familiar edges.

I'll confess, I don't really care for the time between Thanksgiving and Christmas much anyway. My mother loved this time of year. I think being a pastor has ruined it for me:

too much planning, too much pressure, too many varied expectations, too much at stake. But this year it seems to me darker than usual.

I know, my grief is old news to you. And it would be nice if my internal wounds – the wounds of the shock, loss, confusion, anger, disappointment, unknowing, and fatigue of these last nine months – had healed in a way to match what should be by now a small, only slightly identifiable surface scar. And every time I talk about any of this, I feel a bit like the man I visited in the hospital one day shortly after he had had surgery. "You're looking good!" I said. "Well, do you want to see my scar," he retorted. I said that wouldn't be necessary. He pulled up his gown to show me anyway.

I don't want to be that man, so I have to trust that what I am feeling about this season, this year in particular, isn't just something I uniquely know. At least some of you must touch the same set of feelings every year when this holiday season rolls around. And there's almost no validation for it.

People call it *depression*. Like being in a funk in the month of December is some kind of illness or abnormality. There, there. Cheer up.

But it's not that.

It's a sort of disorientation. A sense of being displaced. It has the flavor – the tinge – of grief and confusion and anticipation; this place where past, present and future don't just touch, but collide.

Here's the strange confluence: A sense that this has never happened to me before and this happens to me all the time. Unfamiliar feelings in an always familiar season. It should be this...but instead it is something else. What is it?

Monday, December 22, 2008

Karin,

Dad has Christmas cookies at his house to share with you. I hope you will enjoy some of the favorites that Loyce made from Mom's recipes, including Sand Tarts and Cream Wafers.

The tree is up at Dad's house as well. Rainer and I went on Saturday after the ice storm to cut it, which was really our only opportunity. All the trees were coated with two inches of ice on one side. It was so heavy we could barely get it in the van. Several days of defrosting, using hair dryers and such, meant we could finally take it over today. Decorations are in bins on the high shelves along the wall of the garage as well as in the attic.

Some time we need to talk about the recent visit with the neurologist and his agreement with Dad that he could drive. In the meantime, I have said that he shouldn't drive while there is any ice or snow on the ground and streets, or before he and I can take some practice trips around town. I hope to talk to you sometime soon.

love,
Kurt

Tuesday, March 3, 2009

Dear Karin and Kevin,

I went to the memorial garden this afternoon for a little while. The memorial marker on the stone wall is now in place with Mom's name, dates of birth and death. I didn't realize it would be there until I saw it, but somehow it was comforting -- maybe just a little tangible reminder of her life when I needed it.

love to you both,
Kurt

GRIEF RETURNS

Friday, March 13, 2009

Dear friends,

Some of you may have heard already about my dad's death today. Apparently he died in his sleep sometime in the early morning hours.

I called him last night to invite him to have lunch with me today, and he said he thought maybe he had the flu, so he would need to take a rain check. I told him to call me late morning to let me know if he was feeling better. I didn't hear from him, and went to see him at noon. I let myself into the house, heard the dialysis cycler machine beeping, and knew something was wrong. He was in bed, in a peaceful sleeping position; likely he had a sudden heart attack. Emergency personnel said they thought he had been dead at least six hours, so he died sometime between 11 pm on Thursday and 6 am on Friday.

It caught me by surprise. About six weeks ago or so he started driving again, he was meeting friends occasionally for lunch, participating more actively at church, and attending some of the kids' sporting events. He did all of this with great enjoyment and gratitude for life. I stopped worrying about him so much. He was really able to finally reclaim his life and he was happy.

My sadness is most of all for my children who finally felt they had gotten their grandfather back. And for me, it's too soon after my mom.

I send my love to all of you, and trust that you will keep us all in your prayers. I'll be in touch as memorial plans develop.

love,
Kurt

Saturday, April 11, 2009

Egon Borgmann Memorial Service Reflections

About ten years ago, I took a trip with my father to Germany and Poland. We visited, among other places, the city of his birth and the town where his family settled as refugees in the spring of 1945, after they had fled west to escape the advancing Russian army.

We planted a seed of closer relationship on that trip, that eventually bore its full fruit in these last twelve months of the daily interactions we shared as he recovered from the car accident that killed my mother in March of 2008. But of all the memorable moments from that trip to Europe, there are two that illustrate what I want to say about my father today.

The first was his answer to a question I asked when we visited landmarks in the city of his birth. His home was gone. His city was no longer German. All trace of his family, wiped away. Our hosts, a young Polish couple, seemed curious about my father's memories of the city as it was in the early and mid-1940's, but so far as they were concerned, he might as well have been making up a fairy tale. While the streets were the same, and some of the buildings remained, they could barely imagine his experience, so far removed it was from theirs. Against this backdrop, I asked my father if he had any sadness or regret. He responded that he was glad that for these Polish young people, this city, the only home they had ever known, was their home. He was glad to visit, but his life had moved on.

The second moment took place in Uelzen, the town where his family settled as refugees in the waning days of the war. Through a series of conversations with people the same generation as my father, we found one of his classmates, and eventually, his old girlfriend. My father had never mentioned this woman before, so I was quite curious when he indicated that he wanted to contact her.

So there we were sitting in this woman's living room with her retired sea captain husband holding his pipe in his hand, and she was going on and on about how good it was to see my father after all this time. And then she pulled some photo albums off the shelf, and there were photos of her and my father as 16 and 17 year olds. To me, it was bizarre, but I looked carefully at the photos.

In one photo my father was standing on the dock ready to board the ship to go to the United States as an exchange student. He did not look sad or worried. He was looking forward. In that moment, he could not yet imagine my mother, their life together, his children and grandchildren. All he really knew was what he was about to leave behind. But for me, that is the image that captures his spirit – in the photo, despite all he is leaving behind and all he does not know about what is ahead, he is looking forward, with openness and anticipation blazing on his face.

My dad looked and lived forward. He was adventurous. Always curious. Willing to take a chance on the future. He was never trapped in tradition or bound by the past.

At times, that was the very quality that made it hard to feel close to him. I often felt in my childhood that although he knew I was there and cared for me, he was more inclined to turn his attention and even his heart toward something beyond me.

It was also the quality, I think, that allowed him to survive a war, to come to America, to live on both coasts of this country, to take his family back to his homeland for a time, to leave corporate America after 20 years to become a college professor, to start his own business, to become a left-leaning Democrat after a lifetime of toeing the Republican line, to surf the internet, to read everything he could get his hands on, to look for new news, to learn everything he could from everyone he met.

And, I think, it is what fueled his battle with pancreatic cancer, his recovery from a near-fatal car accident, his determination to manage his own dialysis, his unwillingness to be paralyzed by grief after the death of his wife, his reclaiming of his own life. He looked and he lived forward.

But something else happened in the last year of his life. This is the best part. He did something I never saw him do before. He happily and gratefully anchored himself to the present moment and the surrounding community. That is to say, he kept living forward, but the forward was no longer *away*, it was *into*.

My relationship with him in this last year was transformed because we shared a new level of intimacy and allegiance and trust and gratitude – first by necessity and finally by choice. I am most grateful that even as he kept moving *forward*, he was still moving *toward* – toward me, toward you, toward community, toward love.

GRIEF AFTERWARDS

Sunday, August 16, 2009

Sermon Excerpt: "Flesh and blood?"

The Jews disputed among themselves, saying, "How can this man give us his flesh to eat?" So Jesus said to them, "Very truly I tell you, unless you eat the flesh of the Son of Man and drink his blood, you have no life in you...those who eat my flesh and drink my blood abide in me, and I in them." –John 6:52-53, 56 (NRSV)

My siblings came for the weekend to start the process of deciding what to do with the contents of my parents' house.

We listed items in each room, or put them in categories, talking about what things meant to each of us, which we each might like to have, and how to divide or dispose of the rest. We decided against selling anything in favor of offering to other family members what we can't use. That way, it's not about the money. It's about sharing. It's about memories.

I'd been over to the house a lot – checking on things, watering plants. But for my sister, who hadn't been there since our dad's memorial service months ago, I wondered: How did it feel to walk into the house?

She said it felt good to walk into a moment and a place where my parents' presence still seems evident. It was comforting to her, reassuring.

Interesting. The distance from 'what once was' to 'what now is' seems greater to me. I no longer sit in my mother's chair or put my face into my father's shirts in his closet to catch a lingering scent. It no longer feels strange that they aren't there when I walk in.

And yet, I knew what she meant. So long as the house and their personal items are still there, something of them still lives in those rooms. The evidence that they lived there – *these particular people* lived there – is still all around. There are things that in combination probably exist nowhere else in the universe.

I know that one day that will no longer be true. We were undoing that combination even as we sorted and scattered. One day, the physical evidence of their presence will be gone.

But I am realizing that when that time comes, it will be okay, because it has all leaned in that direction ever since their deaths. We might handle their favorite things, look at photos, touch their clothing, lie down where they used to sleep, even wear their jewelry. Yet none of that substitutes for flesh and blood. It in no way replicates human touch. Once someone is gone, they are gone. There is no going back. No way to hold them again.

Sometimes there are echoes of flesh and blood: I dreamt the other night that I heard my mother's voice. I've dreamt her voice singing once before, near the anniversary of her death, shortly before my father died. But in this one she was talking to me, and I could hear the particular tone of her voice perfectly. I wasn't sure I could retrieve that sound, but in the deep recesses of my mind, it still lives. It is only an echo, though, not flesh and blood. And I can't command it.

On the other hand, I have several voice mail messages of my father's voice saved on my cell phone – mostly requests for errands or bits of news. It comes closer, but it's not flesh and blood – it's not his real, physical presence.

In John 6, Jesus *is* talking about flesh and blood – his own. He speaks mystically, not literally, about his followers eating his flesh and drinking his blood. Yet it's not "just" a metaphor. There is something about the tangible body and blood; the physical sensations that he wants to lift up.

He wants his followers to understand themselves as part of him; for that, they need to "take him in" to themselves. They must swallow all of what they know, sense, believe, and desire of Jesus. They must find a way to touch him, to hold him, not just think *about* him; they must take in his very essence. It's not enough to agree. We have to ingest.

What is the point of taking him into us? Why do we have to do more than just agree to Christ?

In the context of communion, engaging "the elements" of Christ is a way of pledging ourselves to him and his gospel. I've always thought that we eat and drink because we are loyal. *This is my body given for you. This is my blood given for you. Do this in remembrance of me.* We eat the symbols of Jesus' body and blood as a way of holding up our end of the covenant. We promise we won't forget.

But now I am beginning to conceive of this ingesting, this swallowing, this touching and holding, as less about loyalty and more about love.

What if Jesus invites us (and we desire) to draw his life into ours, take his essence into our being, not because we want to be good followers, but because *we want to be one with him*? It's not unlike a sudden and overwhelming urge to embrace our loved ones. Nothing matters so much at that moment as the enfolding of another. Or maybe it's not unlike the way we wish we could hug and kiss and hold just one more time the ones who have gone from this life.

There is nothing like the body, to put our hands to it, our lips to the cheek, to taste and touch. There is nothing like the physical presence of the beloved.

When my siblings and I went through the house, I became aware that I don't care so much about having things that belonged to my father, as I wish I could cut his hair and trim his beard one more time. Bring him a fresh loaf of bread and watch him cut a piece and eat it. Put my arms around him. Flesh and blood.

Saturday, March 13, 2010

Hi Kurt and Kevin,

First anniversary of Dad's death and his upcoming birthday.

I picked out a card with a chicken dancing to an accordion for Benjamin's birthday today. The accordion part made me think of Dad, remembering him talk about his father playing the accordion. I don't know about the chicken part... I didn't really see a family resemblance. ☺

Anyway, wanted you to know I was thinking of you.

Love,
Karin

Dear Karin and Kevin,

Thought of you both as well. Late afternoon I went over to the house to do a little more work, but mostly just to be there. It just felt empty.

When these anniversaries come around I have this anticipation/dread, but what surprised me yesterday was when

I took off Dad's ring just to look at it (which I never do) and realized that this coming June would have been their 50th wedding anniversary. Suddenly I had another whole set of feelings...

I miss you both.
Kurt

Kurt and Karin,

Thanks for your notes. Both made me smile and brought tears to my eyes as well. I still think of Mom and Dad very often – Mom at "special" family gatherings or when I am reading to one of my kids or they are reading to me. Dad, when I am reading the paper and drinking my coffee or when Avery or Walker ask me to explain an adult topic like "how does insurance work?"

Love to you both.
Kevin

Wednesday, June 9, 2010

Reflections for Congregational Luncheon

I've had a couple of perfect moments recently. Do you know what I mean by perfect moments? A perfect moment (as I am wanting to define it) is a moment where something exceedingly valuable comes into view; something pure, something holy. And for a moment, or maybe an hour, you can see life with complete and utter clarity, you know without a doubt what matters, you feel deep and warming gratitude, you feel privileged to be exactly where you are, and you know, as the song we sang through Lent this past spring says, that "All will be well."

So, I've had a couple of these moments recently, and I want to tell you about one: I was pushing Leyna on the swing that hangs from a high tree branch in our back yard. It is high enough and the ropes long enough, that if I really push her as high as she can go, the peak of the swinging potion will take her several feet higher than my head. It's great fun. So, there we were in the back yard and I was pushing her on the swing, and she was calling out "Higher, push me higher!" and I gave her a mighty push, extending my arms and hands out straight and....one of my rings flew off my finger. Not my wedding ring which I wear on my left hand, but my father's wedding ring which I had been wearing on my right hand.

When my father died, I started wearing his ring. His fingers were much larger than mine, so I had it sized down slightly. I've been wearing it ever since. But over the last couple of months, I've been watching my calories and increasing my exercise and I've lost a good bit of weight, and apparently my fingers have gotten thin enough that when I pushed as hard as I could and stretched my hand straight out, the ring just flew off into the yard.

I knew it as soon as it happened. And I stopped the swing and Leyna got down and we started looking. And almost right away I found it. Just the way the sunlight was angled made it shine.

I took it in to the Studio Jewelry Store a couple days later and asked if it could be sized down again, but it can't because it would ruin the engraving inside, so I can't wear it any more.

But here's how it was a perfect moment: It was time to take off the ring, but I don't know that I could have done it myself. How do you stop something you've been doing? Something that symbolizes a moment, a loss, a change in your life? Can you just stop grieving your parents? No you can't. But what could have been a more perfect way for me to stop wearing that ring, to move on, than to have it fly off my finger while pushing my daughter high on a swing while she squeals with delight?

Friday, March 4, 2011

Karin and Kevin,

Yesterday was the anniversary of Mom's death. I wanted to talk to someone about how I was astonished that three years have passed. Then, this morning, I dreamed about Dad.

In the dream, he had just been discharged from the hospital and he came to some sort of gathering I was at. He started engaging people and somehow the conversation turned to skiing. So, he told them he would show them how to ski. He put on his orange coat and his brown speckled winter hat, and went outside with everyone trailing behind, strapped on skis and headed down a gentle slope.

Then, in my dream, some doctors and nurses got wind of what was going on and came running down the street to stop him, but he just skied away, raising his one ski pole in the air triumphantly. I was watching him and smiling when the alarm went off and I woke up. I woke up smiling, too.

I realized that while every now and then I can visit Dad in my dreams, it is much harder for me to find Mom. I wonder if maybe the last year of Dad's life somehow intensified him in my subconscious mind.

love to you both,

Kurt

Hi, Kurt,

I, too, was thinking about Mom yesterday, though I find it more difficult to trace her in the way that I do Dad. We are finishing the last jars of strawberry jam. Also, I am unpacking box upon box of her cookbooks. Cooking and baking must have consumed a great deal of her time. I can see all the recipes she collected from magazines (remember her stacks of magazines in the family room?), her notes about which ones were good and recipes she traded. Her identity was very much wrapped up in things that are a bit foreign to me. Then there was her investment in each of her children and grandchildren. Not all that well executed at times, but there is evidence of that everywhere as well. I see much of that in myself as a mother. Hope to get a chance to talk more later...

Love,

Karin

Sunday, April 8, 2012, Easter Sunday

Sermon Excerpt: "On past death"

But he said to them, "Do not be alarmed; you are looking for Jesus of Nazareth, who was crucified. He has been raised; he is not here. Look, there is the place they laid him. But go, tell his disciples and Peter that he is going ahead of you to Galilee; there you will see him just as he told you." —Mark 16:6-7 (NRSV)

It is easy for us to forget how it must have been for them there at the empty tomb that day, because on Easter morning we are expected to be joyful. We see color, feel warmth, greet the day and each other with *He is risen! He is risen indeed!* We are conditioned to turn in this "good news" direction, a sharp turn from death to life. We *know* how this Easter day is supposed to go. We *know* the tomb is empty and Jesus is alive.

Yet, in "real life," Good Friday doesn't go away that quickly, especially if we are anything like the three women, still waiting and wanting to see Jesus (or any loved one) again, to touch him, to have him back in our arms, if even for a moment, if even in death. The empty tomb is offered as proof that Jesus is risen from the dead. But it's negative proof, right? He should be there, but he isn't, so he must be alive? The women couldn't turn that corner that quickly. That morning, early in the morning, they were looking for his *body*, and the absence of his body just made them even more afraid and even more sad.

That makes sense, because it takes time to move *on past death*. It takes time to stop looking in the direction where the person vanished, and instead move in the direction where they are alive again. It takes time to stop thinking 'tomb thoughts' and to start thinking 'life-goes-on' thoughts. It takes time to stop yearning for what once was (and will no longer be) and to lean in the direction of what is yet to come, what might yet be. An empty tomb is just the beginning. It's the U-turn; it's not the destination.

My mother died at the beginning of March. Near the end of June, at her memorial service, I spoke of her vanishing, but I also told a story about how picking strawberries shifted my grief to the exact opposite – a sense of something of her appearing.

And that's when Easter finally comes – when we can move from this sense that someone has vanished, to this alternate sense that they are re-appearing, and so we know with unexpected and yet reassuring and delightful certainty that truly there *is* something on past death – something healing, something hopeful.

That's why Easter didn't really happen for those three women at the tomb *that* morning, when they were still caught in the confusion of his vanishing. Easter was later for them. It was when Jesus re-appeared. It was when the disciples finally gathered the courage to become a community. The empty tomb wasn't proof enough – at least not emotionally. What they needed was to see him again – to see him in his after-resurrection appearances and to see him in each other.

So today may or may not be Easter for you, as well. You might still be looking in the direction of where some precious part of your life, or where some precious person, has vanished. It won't be Easter until you see, somehow, where life once again appears. All the new flowers and budding trees and colored eggs in the world won't make it Easter, if all you can see is an empty tomb, and you haven't any idea where the Beloved has gone.

Here's the good news: When you are ready, you will find him. On past death, you will see him again. You will touch him. When you are ready, you will catch up to him. Because, as the white-robed man sitting there just inside entrance of the tomb told the women, "He *has* been raised; he is not here (in the tomb)…He is going ahead of you."

Go and find him. Go and find Jesus. He's only a little ahead of you. You can catch up. Go and find him. It's the same for all of your encounters with death, for all who have died. They are only a little ahead of you. You will catch up. You can take that to mean that you will die someday too – that you will "catch up" in that way. But you can also take it to mean that those who have died do re-appear. They have not vanished. They are with us. Just as Jesus is with us.

Jesus appears again and again in our presence, in our lives. How? On past death, is life. *Death does not have the final word.*

Listen again to prophet Isaiah: *The Lord of hosts will destroy on this mountain the shroud that is cast over all peoples, the sheet that is spread over all nations; he will swallow up death forever. Then the Lord will wipe away the tears from all faces…*

And listen again to the angel sitting just inside the empty tomb: *He has been raised; he is not here; he is going ahead of you to Galilee; there you will see him, just as he told you.*

Death does not swallow us up. Death *is* swallowed up. Those we have loved do not vanish forever. Again, they come to us and we to them. Again we touch their lives and they touch ours. Death does not have the final word. It is life that prevails. On past death, is life.

Now – not four months, but four years later – I am seeing my mother more often than in those early weeks and months after her death. Sometimes I hear her voice, her singing even, in my dreams. Sometimes I am caught by a clear understanding of what she would think about something or what she would say. Two weeks ago, plants that were part of the worship center on the communion table at her memorial service, flowers we then planted around the house, started to come up again – splashes of pink and purple. The other day, standing in the kitchen, I looked over at the shelf with the cookbooks on it. One booklet peeked above the others. The recipe showing on the first page of that booklet was her Sunday Morning Coffeecake recipe, written in her still familiar looping handwriting. You know what I am talking about. It happens to you too; these reappearances.

And in the case of Jesus, it's happening all the time, *everywhere* we look: acts of compassion, clear and careful teaching, advocacy for peace, ministry to the poor, aloneness without loneliness, prophetic risks, small children welcomed, meals shared with the outcasts, the community of love. Jesus is reappearing, is resurrected all over the place.

Easter is about seeing, encountering life again. It's not just about an empty tomb; it's about the story that continues. It's about the life that reappears when what we expected is gone and we are surprised by what comes next. It's about what happens when we stop fearing death, and we walk through it. It's what happens when tears are finally wiped away, and joy begins to return.

Lent is over, as are the Lenten practices that teach us to face into death and sorrow. Easter is here, and that means an Easter practice: Imagining a time when the tears will come to an end. Because today, we acknowledge that death does not have the last word. Life goes on.

When you are ready, wrap your arms, wrap your heart, around this good news: That on past death is life.

Sunday, June 5, 2012

Sermon Excerpt: "Holy, Holy, Holy"

Holy, holy, holy is the Lord of hosts; The whole earth is full of his glory. The pivots on the thresholds shook at the voices of those who called. And the house filled with smoke. —Isaiah 6:1-8 (NRSV)

L ast summer when I was on sabbatical, I spent several days at Pendle Hill, the Quaker center on the edge of Philadelphia. The presenter was Miriam Greenspan, a therapist and author from Boston. She had us practice a lot of spiritual and mental exercises as we leaned into the theme, "Healing through the Dark Emotions." One afternoon she led us on a guided meditation that included closing our eyes, listening to a description of a scene, and then following the path that our own minds and hearts led us in response.

Near the end of the meditation, she instructed us to imagine someone important to you approaching with a box. "The box contains something for you," Miriam said. "You open it. What is in it?" She suggested that whatever was in the box symbolized our fears or maybe our hopes.

I felt myself resisting at first, but I gave myself over to imagining the box, even though it's a strange sensation to be creating something in your own mind, without yet knowing what it will be.

In my vision, my parents were the ones who appeared and gave me the box. Out of the box came thick, gray smoke, swirling around me, thicker and thicker, until I could see no shapes, no forms, not even light. And then –strange vision– I discovered that I could breathe! Surrounded by thick smoke, I could still breathe. I heard my parents say, "We're still here. You're okay. Just wait." Finally the smoke cleared, and my parents were still there, dancing together.

Understand the significance of this vision – first, I am allergic enough that with just a small bit of smoke, I feel I can't breathe. That sensation scares me. But in the vision I *could* breathe. And, second, more than anything, my parents loved to dance. For them there was nothing like a waltz around the room in each other's arms. It was complete harmony for them, wholeness.

When I "came back" to the present moment, I found myself surprised by tears and by a sense of being cleansed, at peace. Again, something had shifted, washed away, blown away. It was without a doubt a Spirit-moment. And I won't forget it.

Holy, holy, holy is the Lord of hosts; The whole earth is full of his glory. The pivots on the thresholds shook at the voices of those who called. And the house filled with smoke.

We know holiness when we see it; we know the "Godness" of a moment or a space or a being. We know our own sin, our guilt, our own sense of unworthiness, our own means of cleansing and purifying, our renewed calling. We know these things, and we are restored in the presence of the sacred, the holy. Restored, released, and sent on.

Sunday, August 4, 2013

Sermon Excerpt: "Abundant Life"

And he said to them, "Take care! Be on your guard against all kinds of greed; for one's life does not consist in the abundance of possessions."
–Luke 12:15 (NRSV)

This past weekend, while the town-wide garage sale was advertised in the newspaper to include at least 60 places and participants throughout our town, it seemed to me that many of the bargains were for sale in *my* garage. While we made some money unloading…uh, I mean "selling"…our things to other people, the main goal was to get rid of our excess stuff.

As we organized for the sale, I took a crack at really cleaning out the garage. In the middle of all that stuff were three bins of things cleared from my parents' house after my father's death more than four years ago -- things we'd decided to sort through later, things that document a life.

I threw some things away and others I set aside for my siblings, but at the end of the day, I still had a bin full of the things I couldn't quite throw away. No one would pay anything for these things, but they offer a testimony to lives lived, decisions made, commitments upheld, relationships nurtured, struggles weathered, goals achieved – and in some cases, not achieved.

Going through those three bins really put the rest of the garage sale into perspective. All those tables of things that we put out for sale in the garage versus one plastic bin for keeps; all that stuff that really means nothing to me at all, compared to just one bin of things I couldn't bear to let go.

In Luke's Gospel, Jesus is confronted by a person who wants him to arbitrate the division of a family inheritance. This person likely is the one who is holding the short end of the stick, the one who is not entitled to the family inheritance according to the tradition. He's the underdog, and so perhaps he thinks that Jesus, the champion of the disenfranchised, will come to his aid. But Jesus declines. "Be on guard against all kinds of greed," he says instead, "for one's life does not consist in the abundance of possessions."

I know full well that I am not the sum of what I own, any more than my safety or my well-being is guaranteed by my possessions. I may have a lot of stuff, but I don't imagine that I "can take it with me."

Even though I'm not inclined (like the character in the parable) to build bigger barns and say to my soul, "Soul, you have ample goods laid up for many years; relax, eat, drink, be merry," that doesn't mean that I am immune to the human tendency to misidentify what "treasure" really is. And I certainly am prone to holding on to *stuff.*

Is my treasure the stuff that has monetary value or simply the stuff I hold dear? Is my sense of security based on having "enough" so I don't worry about being unprepared, or is it rooted in something else? What *is* the anchor of my overall sense of well-being? The quality of my relationships? My good health? Time that is my own? The conveniences of life? Is "abundance" about having plenty of all those things?

So what *is* my best "stuff" and how much do I trust in it?

In this scripture, Jesus is less about healing and comfort than he is about warning: Don't measure your security or your well-being in "grain or goods," he says. An abundance of possessions doesn't mean a thing if your life is demanded of you. Instead, travel light. Invest less in *things* and more in…what?

If abundant life is not found in possessions, then where? What *is* the abundant life?

I found some clues sorting through bins in the garage: I thought my desire to hold on was just about trying to secure my memories, yet every single thing I wanted to keep spoke in some way of relationship – of love, or friendship, or good company; of community, of covenant, of togetherness, of moments of connection and closeness: Love letters, worship bulletins, yearbooks, family reunion photos. It became clear to me as I dug through those boxes that what I was sorting through weren't memories so much as symbols; reminders that abundance is not to be found in the *things* we own; it is in the *connections* we make. Abundant life is always rooted in love.

But there's another thing Jesus hints at when he says, "This very night your life is being demanded of you. And the things you have prepared, whose will they be?" While the abundant life may be rooted in love, it is at the same time always slipping through your fingers.

The richest things cannot be possessed or preserved, so much as they are experienced, and in the moment they are experienced, can transport us to a higher plane of wonder or a deeper place of gratitude. Those symbols in those bins – they remind me of treasured experiences – but they are not the same thing as those good moments themselves. They are only an echo. The abundance was in the moment itself.

GRIEF VISITS AGAIN

Monday, March 3, 2014

I knew I wouldn't be myself today. I dread this anniversary every year, but this time it falls on Monday, the same day of the week my mother died, so I knew this particular day would be hard.

It didn't help that this past weekend, I had two more visitations of loss. On Friday, the zipper broke on the blue L.L. Bean jacket that was my father's, the jacket that, when I duck my chin down and to the side, I think I can catch just the faintest scent of him. It can't be fixed, so I can't wear it any more.

And on Saturday, I took from the freezer the last jar of strawberry jam my mother made before she died.

Hanging up my father's jacket and setting out the last jar of rationed jam remind me that I am still deeply sad. We all know that scent and taste are powerful gateways to emotional memories, and when those are gone, something of that memory is lost as well.

I am sad that my parents, who were so often difficult people for me to deal with in recent years, aren't here to deal with anymore. I am sad that no one else seems aware that this is the anniversary. No one has said anything about it to me today. I know the date is etched into my memory in a way that it is not etched into others' memories, so it's not their fault. But still it makes me sad.

There is still some anger, too. I'm frustrated that grief doesn't go away; that it keeps coming back in unpredictable ways, and at times with surprising intensity. I still feel cheated that on an ordinary, random Monday, I walked out of my parents' house with a casual goodbye and I never saw my mother again, and that a year later, just when my father felt he had finally gotten his life back, he, too, was suddenly gone.

I know it's been six years and life goes on. I know that other people expect the sadness to have passed and that it's not rational to be angry about these things, but today I also know I am not finished with my grief.

Monday, March 3, 2014, Late Evening

Feeling a bit sad all day today, as I always do on March 3. Can't believe how the time has passed. In other ways it still seems so close. Grateful the two of you are in my life.

Love,

Kurt

I was thinking the same thing. The year tells us that it was a long time ago and so many things have happened, particularly in our children's lives. On the other hand it feels like time stands still in reference to the important people in our lives.

Love,

Karin

Thanks for your notes. Have been thinking about Mom and Dad a lot this week as a colleague of mine just lost her second parent in a year. Brought back a lot of memories. Love to you both.

Kevin

KURT BORGMANN

GRIEF FORWARD

Sunday, April 5, 2015, Easter Sunday

Sermon Excerpt: "Death swallowed up; Tears wiped away"

He will swallow up death forever. Then the Lord will wipe away tears from all faces, and the disgrace of his people he will take away from all the earth, for the Lord has spoken. —Isaiah 25:8 (NRSV)

I miss my parents more now than I did a year or two after they died, in 2008 and 2009, respectively. I hold my breath through every March, the anniversary month of their deaths. I feel more shadowed by their deaths than held by the spirit of their lives. It seems instead that *death* is not swallowed up, but is swallowing *me* up – one loss at a time. My grief changes, but it does not end.

Make no mistake, I *want* to walk in the direction of Easter resurrection. I'm willing to tie myself to Isaiah's promise: death swallowed up forever; tears wiped away from all our faces. But resurrection is a hard sell for me experientially and emotionally. I *believe* it, but I'm not so sure I *feel* it. Maybe I'm not mature enough in my faith, or maybe I just think too much.

The older I get, the more I'm aware that there are no do-overs, no re-starts, and no going back. Something begins, it lives for a while, and it ends.

I don't mean to rain on the Easter parade. It's just that I need the parade to be real, and my reality has more death in it than resurrection; more tears that *don't* get wiped away than tears that *do*.

So how does the promise of resurrection live in us, when the shadow of death is still so deep and chilling?

I identify with Mary, a realist who showed up at the cemetery expecting a corpse. When it wasn't there, her first thought wasn't resurrection – it was theft. Or someone's cruel joke. Not "A miracle must have happened!" but rather, "Alright, who's taken the body?"

And then, tears spring to her eyes. Because the body is gone? Yes and no. Finding the tomb empty is what *triggers* her crying, but she weeps because it's the final straw. She knows the whole sad story: the betrayal of Jesus by one of his disciples and the abandonment by all the others; she's witnessed the scourging, the mocking, the agony, the death. And it's all too much.

But she's also crying because death has taken this *person* – the touch, the warmth, the words – and robbed her of the future she imagined, expected, hoped for with Jesus. We experience that profound loss, too. So of course, we weep.

But then the story takes a surprising, confusing (and ultimately wondrous), turn: Outside the tomb, Mary encounters Jesus come back from the dead. It's not like time traveling back to what was. He's Jesus, yes, but it isn't a rewind; it's this weird and brilliant and startling leap forward.

Is this what she wants?

I'm not sure, yet she does not turn away from this new Jesus, this now-Christ. She reaches for him, says "Teacher!" In this story, death becomes a passageway to something new. It's not a thief. It's a doorway.

In his essay about dementia and resurrection, writer Samuel Wells highlights the Greek verb *luo* — "I loose." It's the word that means *untying* oxen (Luke 13:15), the *unbinding* of Lazarus from the burial clothes (John 11:44), *breaking down* the walls of hostility (Ephesians 2:14), and *being freed* from sins (Revelation 1:5). *Luo* – I loose, I untie, I unbind, I break free, I let loose. It's a little verb with a lot to offer. "In the face of deficit, decline and death," Wells says, "we try hard to cling on.

But the lesson of that little word *luo* is that the path of resurrection lies in letting go."

This next line was the part that stopped me in my tracks: "If death is starting now (which is the reality which we would say people dealing with dementia are forced to face) then maybe resurrection can start now too. Perhaps it is only when we let go of who and what our loved one was, that we can receive who they are now."

In order to get to resurrection, we have to *release* ourselves, our loved ones. But releasing to death isn't empowering it, giving it the last word – it's moving beyond it. By allowing things to be what they are now, we are given new life, resurrected life – not in the life that was, but in the life that is.

I often think that the wisdom of letting go – of control, of assumptions, of the need for things to be the way I want or expect them to be – is an underutilized spiritual practice. And what if 'letting go' is only the first of two connected steps on the path toward resurrection: letting go of what was *and* receiving what is?

If I'm honest, I don't want to let go of who my loved ones were, so I paint myself into the impossible corner of not being able to receive who they are now. When I think about my parents, for example, with sad and wishful longing, I am imagining transporting them from the way they were *then* into my life *now*, and such a picture is completely false.

It's a tremendous emotional and psychological and spiritual challenge to release that to which we have staked our hearts. Who wants a "new life" when you are perfectly satisfied with the old one? Who wants Christ, when you were happy enough with Jesus?

Mary sees the risen Christ by the empty tomb and she gets it. When she says to the others, "I have seen the Lord," she isn't talking about going back to the Jesus she knew. And this "new" life does not frighten her. It emboldens her. Now she knows death is not a barrier; it's a passage to the other side.

Letting go of who and what our loved one was in order to receive who they are now is about more than death. It can release the care-giver of the person with dementia, the parent of the graduating senior, the dear friend moving away, or someone forced to give up mobility and independence. In each case, something has changed; in fact, died – the person who was, is no more.

The practice of letting go when we don't want to, amounts to training in resurrection, according to Wells. It's an opportunity to experience being changed, and at the same time still recognizably ourselves. Taken up that way, the task becomes less one of resistance than release, recognition, and finally resurrection. And to the ones standing by, thinking mostly of what they are losing or have lost, he offers this thought: "Maybe our loved ones are moving into something new."

On that Easter morning, both Mary and Jesus are moving into something new. It's not the "new" they were expecting, or maybe even desiring, but that doesn't make it hopeless or impossible – just new.

Believing in resurrection is just another way of saying, "I believe that there's always something new…and so I'm not going to cling to the old." And in that sense, death – the thief who takes away what was – cannot overwhelm us or "swallow" us.

There are lots of days I just want to freeze time or turn back the clock. But when I try to live backwards in time, I am living paralyzed, permitting death a continuing hold on me, instead of granting life its inevitable movement toward the possibility of new life. Resurrection is letting the river flow. Life is always lived forward. Death can't change that. That's the promise.

Isaiah says death will be swallowed up and tears will be wiped away. Yes. Not in an instant, but yes. Life is unstoppable. God's love is eternal. Hope is renewed. If we can unclench our fists, unlock our hearts, and let those we love simply be who they are *now* (whether in this world or the next), then we will move into something new; into a resurrected life.

POSTSCRIPT

A book may end, but the story does not. I am certain there are many more chapters yet to be written, and this, I understand, is the way grief is. It does indeed continue to unfold across the weeks, months and years of our lives.

In the spring of 2011, I took a sabbatical with the theme "Gifts of Grief." Upon my return to my congregation, I reported to them my discoveries and insights. Many of the things I learned those three months were not new, but suddenly clear – things like, "This day will never come again," and "We are more resilient than we think," and "We are not alone; everyone is coping with their own losses," and "Nobody's grief is quite like anybody else's," and "People we care about are always leaving us - it's a fact of life."

The last two insights of my sabbatical were these: "Tears come when they will," and "Gratitude is the answer."

I continue to live with those two truths especially and I invite you to do the same: surrender when you must and give thanks at all times.

And may your heart continue to heal.

KURT BORGMANN

ACKNOWLEDGMENTS

I want to offer my thanks to all the persons who have helped me move this project from idea to print.

I am grateful to those who read drafts of the book at various stages, offering first encouragement, and then advice, including James Lehman, Karen Eberly and Bonnie Kline Smeltzer.

I am especially grateful to my editor, Lani Wright. Lani, you've taken me farther than I could have ever traveled on my own.

I want to thank Britta Gene Eberly Glass for her amazing art work that graces the cover of this book, and Klancey Zubowski who brought her considerable design skills to cover and content. Klancey, we know grief, you and I, and we've made it through.

I also owe a great debt of gratitude to the Manchester Church of the Brethren. Much of what I have written here was discerned and expressed in their presence. They were patient and kind to me, especially as I expressed my grief to them in private moments as well as in the pulpit. What a gift this community has been to me.

And finally I offer my deep, deep thanks to my whole family. I am thankful to my siblings, Karin and Kevin Borgmann, not only sister and brother to me, but dear friends to me as well. We've been on this journey together, and I am grateful we continue to accompany each other with love and trust. And to my children, Rainer, Konrad and Leyna, and my wife, Loyce: You mean everything to me and your love sustains me in all times.

Sandra O. Borgmann

Sandra Elizabeth Over was born July 30, 1938 in Roaring Spring, PA, to Robert S. Over and Mildred Hoover Over.

Sandra was a graduate of Roaring Spring High School, class of 1956. It was during high school that she met her future husband, Egon Borgmann. He was an exchange student from Germany living for a year with Carl and Doreen Myers. Carl was the pastor of Sandra's church (Roaring Spring First Church of the Brethren) and Sandra was the baby sitter to Carl and Doreen's young children. Immediately after graduating, Sandra participated in a work camp to Germany sponsored by the Church of the Brethren. There she was reunited with Egon. He later emigrated to the United States.

Sandra completed her undergraduate degree at Juniata College in 1960 and married Egon on June 25 of that same year. She also completed post-graduate course work in Elementary Education at Temple University. She was an elementary school teacher in the Upper Darby (PA) School District and later committed her energies to raising her three children, Karin, Kurt, and Kevin.

Active in the church her entire life, she was at various times a member of the Roaring Spring First Church of the Brethren, Trinity Presbyterian Church and the Wilmington Church of the Brethren in Wilmington, DE, and after moving to North Manchester, IN, the Manchester Church of the Brethren.

Sandra was the beloved "Grammy" of seven grandchildren. She enjoyed attending and supporting her grandchildren's sports and school activities, gardening, cross-stitching, and baking pies and prolific numbers of Christmas cookies to share with her family and friends.

She was preceded in death by her parents. She is survived by her husband, her children and grandchildren, and two brothers.

Egon W. H. Borgmann

Egon W. H. Borgmann, 72, North Manchester, IN, died at 6:00 a.m., Friday, March 13, 2009 at his home. Over the last year he had overcome a series of obstacles in his recovery from injuries sustained in an auto accident in March 2008, and had reclaimed his life and place in the community.

He was born March 16, 1936 in Stettin, Germany, resettling with his family in Uelzen, Germany, in 1945 as a war refugee. He came to the United States as an exchange student in 1953 where he stayed with the family of Carl and Doreen Myers in Roaring Spring, PA. There he met his future wife, Sandra Over. After returning to Germany and serving an apprenticeship in Import/Export, he immigrated to the United States. He married Sandra on June 25, 1960.

He subsequently graduated from Temple University and received an M.B.A. from the Wharton School at the University of Pennsylvania. He worked for the DuPont Company in Wilmington, Delaware before committing his energies to starting his own business in international marketing and teaching in the business program at Ursinus College. Most recently he worked as the Finance Director at the Red Cross of the Delmarva Peninsula.

After retirement, he moved with his wife Sandra to North Manchester, IN where he was an active member of the Manchester Church of the Brethren. He was the beloved and courageous father of three children and grandfather of seven grandchildren. He enjoyed soccer, canoeing, hiking, reading, and taking on new challenges. He was preceded in death by his wife of 48 years, Sandra Borgmann, and his parents, Margarete and Walter Borgmann.

He is survived by his children, his grandchildren, and a sister.

ABOUT THE AUTHOR

Kurt Borgmann is a pastor in the Church of the Brethren. He has served congregations in Illinois, Florida, Virginia and Indiana. His current congregation is the Manchester Church of the Brethren, in North Manchester, Indiana.

Made in the USA
Lexington, KY
27 October 2015